Your Subconscious Awakening

Unleash Your Mind's Hidden Potential

Deepak Singh

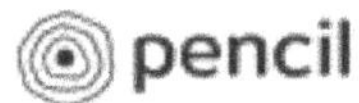

ISBN 978-93-5667-697-8
© Deepak Singh 2023

Published in India 2023 by Pencil

A brand of
One Point Six Technologies Pvt. Ltd.
Unit no. 26, Ground Floor, Building A1,
Wadala Truck Terminal Road,
Near Post Office, Antop Hill, Mumbai - 400037
E connect@thepencilapp.com
W www.thepencilapp.com

Author biography

Hello! Happy to meet you, I'm Deepak Singh. I work as a research analyst and am passionate about writing books and doing research on the planet Earth, space, and the art of living. I most likely have high analytical and critical thinking abilities that enable me to assess data, spot trends, and reach conclusions in my capacity as a research analyst. As part of my job, I might perform primary and secondary research, analyze available data, and provide findings to guide individual, corporate, or organizational decision-making. I adore writing and researching as interests in space and Earth in my free time. You can tell that I have an open mind and am interested in learning about the world around you.

CONTENTS

Introduction

In this book, we will look at the subconscious mind and its significance in our lives. We'll talk about how the subconscious mind operates and how it interacts with the conscious mind. We'll also look at how the subconscious mind influences our actions, ideas, and emotions.

Your subconscious mind is the most powerful instrument you possess. It holds the secret to realizing your full potential, attaining your goals, and living the life you want. However, most of us are unaware of our subconscious mind's power, and as a result, we limit ourselves and struggle to live the life we desire.

In "Your Subconscious Awakening," we will look at the power of your subconscious mind and how to awaken it in order to make positive changes in your life. We will go into the subconscious mind, revealing the programming that has been holding you back and restricting your potential. Affirmations, visualizations, and guided meditations will be discussed as approaches for reprogramming the subconscious mind.

We will also look at how mindfulness and self-awareness might help to awaken the subconscious mind. We'll talk about how dreams play a part in the subconscious mind and how they may be used as a tool for self-discovery. We will also look at how to cure the subconscious mind and how to develop happy subconscious thinking.

By the end of this book, you will have a thorough understanding of your subconscious mind's power and how to use it to make positive changes in your life. You'll have a toolbox full of tools for reprogramming your subconscious mind, healing old traumas, and cultivating a good mindset. You will be empowered to take charge of your life and design the life you want.

Chapter 1 Understanding the Subconscious Mind

We shall go deeper into the workings of the subconscious mind in this chapter. We'll look at the various layers of the subconscious mind and how they affect our behavior. We will also look at the various forms of programming stored in the subconscious mind and how they affect our life.

For ages, philosophers, biologists, and psychologists have been fascinated by the human mind, which is a complicated and intriguing creature. The subconscious mind is one element of the mind that has sparked considerable curiosity. While most people have heard the word "subconscious," few actually comprehend what it entails and how it influences our ideas, behaviors, and overall well-being. In this post, we'll go deeper into the subconscious mind, learning what it is, how it functions, and how we might harness its power.

What exactly is the Subconscious Mind?

The subconscious mind is part of our mind that is not immediately visible to our conscious awareness. It's in charge of our automatic behaviors, routines, and reactions. The subconscious mind functions beneath conscious consciousness and is in charge of digesting and storing all of the information we are exposed to on a daily basis. Everything from our memories and beliefs to our emotions and instincts is included.

Even when we are not actively paying attention, our subconscious mind is constantly digesting information from our environment. It uses this data to modify our thoughts, feelings, and behaviors, frequently without our knowledge. For example, if we see a particular brand of soda advertised repeatedly, our subconscious mind may acquire a liking for that brand, even though we are not consciously aware of it.

What Is the Function of the Subconscious Mind?

The subconscious mind is a potent force that operates outside of our conscious awareness. It is continually processing information and impacting our ideas, behaviors, and emotions in the background. Our automatic biological activities, such as breathing, heartbeat, and digestion, are also controlled by the subconscious mind.

The ability of the subconscious mind to store and recall information is one of its most significant roles. When we learn anything new, the conscious mind processes the information first. However, continuous exposure progressively transfers the information to the subconscious mind, where it can be accessed quickly and efficiently. This is why we can accomplish certain things, such as driving or typing, without having to think about it.

Our emotional responses are also controlled by the subconscious mind. The subconscious mind is in charge of our emotions, and our emotional responses frequently impact our thoughts and behaviors. For example, if we are terrified of spiders, our subconscious mind may cause us to feel anxious or panicked when we see one.

The subconscious mind is in charge of digesting information that our conscious mind does not have access to. It is the section of the brain that holds our memories, emotions, beliefs, and routines. It also controls our natural responses, such as fight or flight, and is in charge of basic activities like breathing and digestion.

One of the subconscious mind's most crucial functions is to keep us safe. It accomplishes this by constantly evaluating the environment for potential threats and, when necessary, activating our fight-or-flight response. This response is critical for our survival because it helps us to respond swiftly in harmful situations. However, if it is activated too frequently or unintentionally, it can cause anxiety and stress.

The subconscious mind is extremely important in shaping our thoughts and values. Our views and values emerge early in life and are shaped by our surroundings, experiences, and relationships. These beliefs and values are stored in the subconscious mind and used to influence our thoughts and behavior. Depending on the thoughts and ideals we have internalized, this might be positive or detrimental.

For example, if we believe we are not good enough, our subconscious mind will repeatedly reinforce that attitude, resulting in negative self-talk and low self-esteem. On the other hand, if we believe that we can accomplish anything we set our minds to, our subconscious mind will seek to reinforce that view, resulting in positive self-talk and improved confidence.

Our habits and instinctive behaviours are also controlled by the subconscious mind. Habits are actions that we do without thinking, such as brushing our teeth or driving a car. These habits are created and stored in the subconscious mind through repetition. When we create a habit, it becomes automatic, and we no longer have to think about it.

However, habits can be both beneficial and detrimental. Positive habits like regular exercise and a healthy diet can enhance our lives and well-being. Negative habits, such as smoking and overeating, can be harmful to our health and happiness. The subconscious mind is in charge of both habit formation and habit breaking. We may reprogram our habits and make positive changes in our lives by modifying our subconscious ideas and ideals.

Our creativity and intuition are also influenced by our subconscious mind. Intuition is the ability to understand something instinctively, without the need for conscious reasoning. Creativity is the ability to come up with fresh and unique ideas. The subconscious mind is responsible for both creativity and intuition.

When we do creative things like painting, writing, or playing music, we enter a state of flow in which our subconscious mind takes over and we become completely absorbed in the job at hand. Our subconscious mind is free to generate connections and associations that our conscious mind may not be able to see in this condition. This might result in novel and creative thoughts and solutions.

Intuition works on a subconscious level as well. When we have a gut feeling about something, it is our subconscious mind sending us a message based on facts that we may or may not be consciously aware of. Trusting our intuition can help us make better decisions and more efficiently navigate the world around us.

To summarise, the subconscious mind is a powerful force that influences our ideas, feelings, and behavior in ways we may be unaware of. It is necessary for our survival, beliefs, habits, creativity, and intuition. Understanding how the subconscious mind works can assist us in harnessing its ability to effect positive change in our lives. We may reprogram our behaviors, increase our creativity, and make better decisions by becoming more aware of our subconscious beliefs and values. Finally, the subconscious mind is an important aspect of our psyche, and by learning to work with it, we may maximize our potential and attain greater levels of success and fulfillment in our lives.

How Can We Harness the Subconscious Mind's Power?

Using the power of the subconscious mind for personal growth and transformation can be a tremendous tool. There are various strategies for accessing and using the power of the subconscious mind.

The subconscious mind is an essential component of our psyche, influencing our ideas, feelings, and behavior. It is the part of the mind that acts below the level of conscious consciousness and is in charge of our automatic responses to various environmental stimuli. Even if we are unaware of its workings, the subconscious mind has a huge impact on our daily lives. In this post, we will look at how the subconscious mind works and how it influences our life.

Meditation is one of the most powerful strategies to gain access to the subconscious mind. Meditation is an extremely effective practice for calming the mind and reaching deeper states of consciousness. We can access the subconscious mind and harness its power by quieting the conscious mind.

Hypnosis is another method for gaining access to the subconscious mind. Hypnosis is a deep relaxation state in which the subconscious mind is more open to suggestions. A professional hypnotherapist can guide an individual into a state of deep relaxation during hypnosis, allowing them to access the subconscious mind and create good changes.

Another method for accessing the power of the subconscious mind is visualization. Visualization entails forming mental images of the desired outcome and focussing on them with intention and belief. We can use the power of the subconscious mind to materialize positive changes in our lives by visualizing positive results.

Finally, the subconscious mind is a potent force that shapes our thoughts, behaviors, and emotions. We can harness its power for personal growth and transformation by tapping into its power through practices such as meditation, hypnosis, and visualization. Understanding our subconscious minds is a necessary step towards realizing our full potential and living our best lives.

Chapter 2 Uncovering Your Subconscious Beliefs

This chapter will go over the significance of uncovering your subconscious beliefs. We'll look at how our ideas influence our lives and how they form our thoughts and actions. We'll also go over methods for identifying and modifying limiting beliefs.

Our beliefs influence our ideas, actions, and, eventually, our lives. Did you know, though, that many of our beliefs are subconscious? These are beliefs that we have without realizing it, and they can have a significant impact on our lives.

Discovering your subconscious beliefs is a critical stage in personal development and self-awareness. Here are some pointers to help you discover your subconscious beliefs:

Pay attention to your inner dialogue: Your inner dialogue might reveal a lot about your underlying views. Take note of the vocabulary you use when talking to yourself. Do you engage in negative self-talk? Do you convince yourself that you're not good enough or that you're incapable of doing something? Negative beliefs can be ingrained in your mind.

The constant conversation that goes on inside your head is known as subconscious inner dialogue, often known as self-talk. It's the voice you hear while you're thinking about something, making a decision, or interacting with others. While you may not be conscious of your inner dialogue all of the time, it has a tremendous impact on your thoughts, feelings, and behavior.

Many people are unaware of the strength of their subconscious inner dialogue. They frequently let it run on autopilot without paying attention to what it's saying. You may, however, begin to harness the power of your self-talk by being more conscious of it.

Here are some suggestions for tuning in to your subconscious inner dialogue:

- **Make a mental note of your thoughts:** Begin paying attention to your thoughts throughout the day. You may be startled to learn how much negative self-talk you engage in without even realizing it. Take note of these thoughts and look for patterns.

- **Confront negative self-talk:**When you catch yourself engaging in negative self-talk, challenge it. Check to see if what you're telling yourself is true. Negative self-talk is frequently based on incorrect assumptions or inaccurate views. You can begin to replace negative self-talk with more positive, empowering ones by challenging it.

- **Make use of positive affirmations:**Affirmations are positive affirmations that you repeat to yourself in order to alter your internal dialogue. If you're battling with self-doubt, for example, you may repeat the affirmation "I am capable and confident." Choose affirmations that speak to you and repeat them to yourself on a daily basis.

- **Exercise mindfulness:**Mindfulness is the practice of being fully present in the present moment. You become more conscious of your thoughts and emotions as you practice mindfulness. This might assist you in identifying and replacing negative self-talk with more positive self-talk.

In conclusion, paying attention to your subconscious inner dialogue can help you become more self-aware and improve your life. By challenging negative self-talk, using positive affirmations, practicing mindfulness, and seeking help if needed, you can start to transform your inner dialogue and cultivate a more positive, empowering mindset.

Determine your triggers: Negative emotions or ideas might be triggered by certain situations or persons. Take notice of what causes these feelings and thoughts. It can assist you in identifying the underlying assumptions that are causing problems.

After you've identified your subconscious triggers, you can start rewiring your subconscious mind. Affirmations, visualization, and meditation are among the practices that can help to replace negative thoughts and routines with good ones.

You can harness the power of your subconscious mind to achieve your objectives and live a more happy life by becoming aware of your subconscious triggers and trying to reprogram your subconscious mind.

Consider your childhood memories: Many of our subconscious beliefs are created while we are children. Consider your early experiences and any views that may have developed during that period. For example, if you grew up in a low-income environment, you may develop subconscious views about scarcity and lack. Childhood is a period of wonder, exploration, and development. It is a stage in life when we build our sense of self and lay the groundwork for our personality and worldview. Childhood memories can have a significant impact on our adult lives, affecting our ideas, feelings, and behaviors.

Our subconscious is a memory bank that we are not always aware of. Smells, noises, or even specific words or phrases can evoke these recollections. Childhood subconscious memories are especially important because they can form our perceptions of the world and of ourselves.

Reflecting on the experiences that stand out in your mind is one technique to examine your childhood subconscious memories. Consider your earliest memories, attempting to recall specific events, people, and feelings. Make a list of anything that comes to mind, no matter how minor it may appear.

Pay attention to any repeating themes or patterns as you reflect on your early experiences. Do you remember feeling terrified or alone, for example? Do you remember feeling loved and supported? These themes can reveal your underlying beliefs and feelings.

It's also vital to think about how your childhood experiences shaped your current attitudes and behaviors. For example, if you were rejected or abandoned as a child, you may battle with feelings of insecurity or poor self-worth as an adult. On the other side, if you had a positive upbringing with kind carers, you may develop a high sense of self-worth and confidence.

Investigating your subconscious childhood memories can be a tremendous tool for personal growth and healing. You can begin to question negative patterns and create a more positive self-image by understanding how your prior experiences have affected your thoughts and feelings. You can learn to love your past and move on with better self-awareness through time, self-reflection, and resilience.

Journaling allows you to examine your thoughts and emotions: Journaling can be an effective strategy for revealing subconscious thoughts. Spend some time every day writing down your ideas and emotions. Be truthful with yourself and investigate any underlying assumptions that may be influencing your thoughts and feelings.

Journaling is a centuries-old practice that has been used to record one's thoughts, experiences, and emotions. While journaling can be utilized for a variety of purposes, one of the most important advantages is the opportunity to investigate your subconscious thoughts and feelings.

Our subconscious mind is a large and powerful repository of information and emotions that we may be completely unaware of. It is the portion of our brain that stores our beliefs, attitudes, and values, and it shapes how we see and interact with the world around us. We may tap into this rich stream of information and develop a better understanding of ourselves by journaling.

When we write in a journal, we enable ourselves to freely and without judgment express our ideas and emotions. We can write about our uncertainties, doubts, and insecurities, as well as our fears, hopes, desires, and aspirations. By doing so, we establish a secure and non-judgmental environment in which to examine our deepest thoughts and feelings.

When we journal, we may uncover patterns in our thoughts and emotions that we were previously unaware of. We may identify reoccurring ideas, beliefs, or attitudes that have been impeding or stressing us. We may begin to grasp the underlying issues that are driving these trends and try to address them by identifying them.

Journaling also assists us in more effectively processing our feelings. We are better equipped to make sense of and put our thoughts into perspective when we write about them. This can assist us in better managing our emotions, lowering stress, and enhancing our general well-being.

Finally, journaling is an effective technique for exploring our subconscious ideas and feelings. We can obtain a better understanding of ourselves and our motivations by creating a secure and non-judgmental environment in which to examine our innermost thoughts and feelings. This, in turn, can help us address underlying difficulties, better control our emotions, and enhance our general well-being.

Seek the assistance of a therapist or coach: If you're having trouble uncovering your subconscious beliefs, consider hiring a therapist or coach. They can assist you in exploring your thoughts and feelings in a safe and supportive setting.

You can work on modifying your subconscious ideas once you've identified them. This can include challenging harmful beliefs, reframing them, and replacing them with more beneficial positive beliefs.

Remember that your beliefs influence your life. You may create a more pleasant and satisfying life for yourself by uncovering and modifying your subconscious beliefs.

Chapter 3 The Power of Positive Affirmations

In this chapter, we will look at the effectiveness of positive affirmations. We'll look at how affirmations can help us reprogram our subconscious minds and use them to attain our goals. We will also look at various ways for producing powerful affirmations.

The human mind is a strong weapon that has the ability to make or shatter our life. Our thoughts and beliefs have the power to mold our world and impact our behavior. Positive affirmations are a powerful technique for harnessing the power of our minds in order to live a positive and fulfilling life.

Positive affirmations are phrases repeated to oneself in order to cultivate a positive mentality and encourage positive thinking. They are simple, yet powerful sentences that can assist us in shifting our emphasis from negative to good ideas. These affirmations can help us overcome negative self-talk, increase our self-esteem, and improve our overall well-being.

An increasing collection of scientific evidence supports the efficacy of positive affirmations. Positive affirmations have been found in studies to help reduce stress, boost mood, and improve general psychological well-being. They can also benefit our physical health by alleviating the symptoms of stress-related disorders like high blood pressure and heart disease.

Positive affirmations work by assisting us in focusing on our goals and believing in ourselves. We train our thoughts to think optimistically and believe in our own skills by repeating positive affirmations. This can assist us in overcoming limiting beliefs and negative self-talk that can prevent us from attaining our goals.

Positive affirmations have been shown to have powerful effects in the realm of psychology. The subconscious mind is a strong force that may be used to assist us in achieving our objectives, overcoming barriers, and living happier, more fulfilled lives.

Positive affirmations are brief, uncomplicated remarks intended to assist us in overcoming negative ideas and attitudes. They can be utilized to alter our perceptions of ourselves and our surroundings, as well as to replace negative thoughts and beliefs with positive ones.

Positive affirmations become deeply buried in our subconscious mind when we repeat them to ourselves on a regular basis. This can have a significant impact on how we think and feel, allowing us to achieve our goals and live the life we want.

Positive affirmations include the following:

- I am deserving of love and respect.

- I am capable of reaching my objectives.

- I follow my instincts and make sound decisions.

- I am thankful for everything nice in my life.

- I am fit and strong.

To get the most out of positive affirmations, we must choose affirmations that speak to us personally. We should also say them frequently, ideally every day, and visualize ourselves achieving our goals as we do so. It can also use to write them down and post them somewhere prominent, such as a mirror or a computer desktop.

Positive affirmations should be repeated on a regular basis, preferably daily, and with conviction and belief. You can say them out or silently to yourself, and writing them down and reading them on a regular basis will assist.
Positive affirmations are extremely effective when used with other self-improvement techniques such as meditation, visualization, and goal setting. You may construct a powerful instrument for attaining your goals and living the life you want by combining these practices.

In conclusion, positive affirmations are a strong tool for improving our thinking, increasing our confidence, and achieving our goals. We may create a more happy and more satisfying existence by training our thoughts to think positively and believe in ourselves. So, the next time you notice yourself thinking badly, try replacing those thoughts with positive affirmations and witness for yourself the power of positive thinking. We may tap into the immense power of our subconscious mind and create the life we genuinely desire by employing positive affirmations on a regular and consistent basis.

Chapter 4 Visualizations and Guided Meditations

In this chapter, we will look at the effectiveness of visualizations and guided meditations. We'll look at how these strategies can help us get into our subconscious minds and make positive changes in our lives. We will also go through several sorts of visualizations and guided meditations, as well as how to use them effectively.

Visualizations and guided meditations are effective methods for improving mental clarity, reducing stress, and improving overall well-being. Mental imaging and concentrated attention are utilized in these practices to create a certain feeling or sensation in the mind and body.

Visualizations are mental images or scenarios that are produced and stored in one's mind. These images can be used to help people achieve a specific end, such as overcoming anxiety or reaching a goal. Someone who is nervous, for example, may utilize a visualization of a peaceful beach to assist them relax and calm their mind.

Guided meditations, on the other hand, are meditations that are structured and guided by a teacher or instructor. Body scans, breathwork exercises, and mindfulness practices are examples of meditations. The instructor will frequently lead the meditator through the practice, providing reminders and suggestions to keep them focused and centered.

Visualizations and guided meditations can both be quite effective at relieving tension and anxiety. We activate the parasympathetic nerve system, which is responsible for the body's "rest and digest" response when we participate in these practices. This can reduce heart rate, blood pressure, and cortisol levels, all of which contribute to stress and anxiety.

Visualizations and guided meditations can help people create better self-awareness and inner calm in addition to reducing stress. We can learn to monitor our thoughts and feelings without judgment by concentrating our attention inward and focusing on the present moment. This will provide us with better clarity and insight into our inner world.

There are numerous sorts of visualizations and guided meditations, each of which is intended to help a specific outcome. A visualization focusing on richness and prosperity, for example, would include envisioning oneself surrounded by wealth and success, whilst a guided meditation for sleep might include progressive muscular relaxation and deep breathing exercises.

One of the most significant advantages of visualizations and guided meditations is that they may be done by anyone, anywhere, at any time. Many materials are available online, including guided meditations and visualizations on YouTube, as well as meditation apps such as Headspace and Calm.

Finally, visualizations and guided meditations are effective tools for stress reduction, self-awareness cultivation, and overall well-being. We can harness the power of the mind-body connection and experience greater calm, clarity, and joy in our life by implementing these practices into our everyday routines.

Chapter 5 Mindfulness and Self-Awareness

In this chapter, we'll talk about how mindfulness and self-awareness can help you awaken your subconscious mind. We will look at how mindfulness and self-awareness can help us identify and overcome undesirable behavioral patterns. We will also look at various approaches to cultivating mindfulness and self-awareness.

Mindfulness and self-awareness are two principles that can help people enhance their general well-being and achieve greater success in life. The practice of being fully present in the moment, aware of one's thoughts, feelings, and surroundings without judgment, is referred to as mindfulness. In contrast, self-awareness refers to the ability to recognize and comprehend one's own thoughts, feelings, and behaviors.

Mindfulness practice can help people develop self-awareness by allowing them to notice their thoughts and feelings without judgment. This can help people become more aware of their emotional patterns and triggers, which can help them make better decisions and respond more effectively to tough situations.

Meditation is one method for practicing mindfulness and developing self-awareness. Meditation entails concentrating one's attention on a single object or experience, such as one's breath while letting go of distractions and judgments. Individuals who practice meditation on a regular basis might become more aware of their thoughts and feelings and gain better control over their reactions to them.

Self-reflection is another approach to practicing mindfulness and self-awareness. Individuals can obtain insight into their own behavior and motivations by taking the time to think about their thoughts, feelings, and actions. Individuals can use this to find areas where they may need to make changes or enhance their skills.

Daily activities such as eating, exercising, or even brushing one's teeth can be used to practice mindfulness and self-awareness. Individuals can acquire more self-awareness and mindfulness in their daily lives by focusing their attention fully on the present moment and being aware of their thoughts and feelings.

There are various advantages to practicing mindfulness and self-awareness. These practices can help people reduce stress and anxiety, improve their attention and concentration, and improve their interpersonal interactions. They can also assist individuals in developing more self-confidence and resilience in the face of adversity.

Finally, mindfulness and self-awareness are critical practices for those who want to improve their general well-being and attain greater success in life. Individuals can gain a greater understanding of themselves and their emotions by cultivating mindfulness and self-awareness through meditation, self-reflection, and daily activities, leading to improved decision-making and a greater sense of inner peace and fulfillment.

Chapter 6 Dream Analysis

We will look at the role of dreams in the subconscious mind in this chapter. We will look at how dreams may be used to aid in self-discovery and provide insights into our subconscious programming. We will also go through several dream analysis approaches.

Humans have long been fascinated with dreams, with numerous theories and interpretations suggested over the years. The notion of subconscious dream analysis, which tries to unearth the hidden meanings underlying the symbols and events in our dreams, is one way to understand dreams.

The premise behind subconscious dream analysis is that our dreams are a representation of our subconscious mind. Our subconscious mind, according to this notion, is responsible for many of our thoughts, feelings, and behaviors, and it interacts with us through dreams.

Dream symbols and occurrences are regarded to be expressions of our subconscious mind, which is frequently attempting to communicate with us. We can obtain insights into our deepest wants, fears, and motives by analyzing these symbols and occurrences.

There are numerous methods for analyzing dreams, but the most prominent are free association, symbol interpretation, and archetypal analysis.

Exploring the numerous links and connections that spring to mind when you think about the symbols and events in your dream is what free association is all about. For example, if you have a dream about a snake, you may freely correlate it with terms such as danger, dread, or temptation. You can acquire a better grasp of what the snake may signify in your dream by investigating these associations.

Symbol interpretation is deciphering the hidden meanings of the many symbols in your dream. This method is frequently based on the notion that certain symbols have universal meanings that transcend cultures and time periods. Water, for example, may represent the unconscious mind or emotions, but a house could represent the self or psyche.

Another approach to dream interpretation is archetype analysis, which focuses on the recurrent patterns and themes that are present in our dreams. These patterns and motifs, according to this view, are archetypes, or universal symbols that are shared across cultures and time periods. The hero archetype, for example, may manifest in your dreams as a brave and daring individual who overcomes hurdles and problems.

Overall, subconscious dream interpretation can be a valuable technique for learning about our deepest wants, anxieties, and motives. We can better understand ourselves and our place in the world by investigating the symbols and events in our dreams. While mastering the skill of dream analysis can take time and practice, the benefits can be really transforming.

Chapter 7 Healing the Subconscious Mind

We will look at ways for repairing the subconscious mind in this chapter. We'll look at how unresolved emotions and traumas can affect the subconscious mind and how to let them go. We will also go through various therapeutic treatments including hypnosis and energy healing.

The human mind is a complicated mechanism that governs our ideas, emotions, and actions. It is split into two parts: the conscious and subconscious minds. The conscious mind is in charge of our daily ideas and activities, but the subconscious mind is in charge of our automatic thoughts, beliefs, and emotions. These automatic ideas and beliefs can have a significant impact on our behavior and can be the basis of many mental health problems. As a result, repairing the subconscious mind is critical for overall well-being.

The subconscious mind is a large library that stores all of our experiences, memories, and beliefs. These memories and beliefs influence our behavior and shape our experience of reality. Negative events, trauma, and unresolved emotions can all result in deeply ingrained beliefs in our subconscious minds that can cause long-term harm. These beliefs can appear in anxiety, sadness, addiction, and other mental health problems.

To cure the subconscious mind, one must first recognize and address the harmful beliefs that have become deeply embedded in it. The first step is to recognize and accept the presence of these ideas. It is critical to understand that these views are not a reflection of one's identity, but rather the result of previous events and indoctrination.

Mindfulness and meditation practices are effective ways to cure the subconscious mind. Mindfulness assists people in becoming more aware of their thoughts and emotions, allowing them to identify and release detrimental ideas. Meditation techniques such as visualization and affirmation can also aid in the reprogramming of the subconscious mind with positive thoughts.

Therapy is another important strategy. Therapy can assist in identifying and addressing ingrained beliefs that may be creating mental health problems. A therapist can assist in understanding the fundamental cause of negative thoughts as well as provide skills to repair and reprogram the subconscious mind.

In addition to treatment, activities that increase self-awareness and self-care can be undertaken. Journaling, art therapy, and physical activity are all excellent strategies to relieve stress and increase general well-being. These activities can assist individuals in connecting with their inner selves, identifying detrimental ideas, and replacing them with positive ones.

Healing the subconscious mind is a slow and steady process that demands patience and dedication. It is critical to remember that healing is not a straight line and that setbacks are a normal part of the process. Even though it is difficult, one must be nice to oneself and continue to work towards recovery.

Finally, repairing the subconscious mind is critical for overall well-being. Negative beliefs and emotions can lead to mental health problems and influence our behavior. Mindfulness, meditation, counseling, and self-care are all excellent methods for healing the subconscious mind. Negative thoughts must be acknowledged and accepted, and one must commit to the healing process. One can reprogram their subconscious mind with positive thoughts and achieve long-term mental and emotional well-being with patience and commitment.

Chapter 8 Creating a Positive Subconscious Mindset

This chapter will go over ways for developing positive subconscious thought. We will look at how our thoughts and emotions affect our subconscious mind, as well as how to create happy thoughts and emotions. We will also look at many approaches for cultivating a good mindset.

The subconscious mind is a powerful force that, depending on how we train it, can work for or against us. When our subconscious mind is cluttered with negative thoughts and beliefs, we tend to see the world through a negative lens, which can be harmful to our mental and emotional well-being. A positive subconscious thought, on the other hand, maybe extremely empowering, assisting us in overcoming problems and achieving our goals. In this post, we will look at several successful methods for developing a good subconscious mindset.

- **Practice Gratitude:**Practising thankfulness is one of the easiest yet most powerful methods to develop a happy subconscious mindset. When we concentrate on what we are grateful for, we educate our thoughts to find the positive in any scenario. Create a thankfulness diary and write down three things you are grateful for each day.

You will discover that your subconscious mind begins to instinctively focus on the good aspects of your life over time.

- **Positive Affirmations:**Affirmations are another effective strategy for developing positive subconscious thinking. These are short, positive words that you tell yourself on a daily basis in order to promote positive thoughts and attitudes. Positive affirmations include phrases like "I am worthy," "I am capable," and "I am deserving of love and happiness." Repeat these affirmations to yourself throughout the day, particularly when you notice yourself thinking negatively

- **Visualization:**Visualisation is a process that involves forming a mental image of the desired goal. When you see yourself successful, your subconscious mind comes to believe that success is attainable. To begin using visualization, locate a quiet spot to sit and close your eyes. Visualize yourself accomplishing your goal as precisely as possible. Consider how you would feel, what you would do, and who you would be with. The stronger the effect on your subconscious mind, the more vivid and detailed your visualization.

- **Surround Yourself with Positive People:**The individuals we spend our time with have a big influence on our subconscious mind. We are more inclined to adopt positive attitudes and beliefs when we surround ourselves with pleasant, helpful people. Spending time with negative people, on the other hand, might encourage negative mental patterns and ideas. Make a concerted effort to surround yourself with individuals that inspire and uplift you.

- **Practice Mindfulness:**Mindfulness is the practice of being fully involved in what you are doing and being present at the moment. We are less likely to become engrossed in negative thoughts and feelings when we are mindful. Mindfulness can be practiced in a variety of methods, such as meditation, yoga, or simply taking a few deep breaths when agitated or concerned. You may teach your subconscious mind to be more present and focused on the present moment by practicing mindfulness on a regular basis.

To summarise, developing a positive subconscious mentality is an effective strategy to improve your mental and emotional well-being, overcome obstacles, and achieve your goals. You may teach your subconscious mind to focus on the good and build a more fulfilling existence by practicing gratitude, positive affirmations, visualization, surrounding yourself with positive people, and practicing mindfulness.

Chapter 9 Putting it All Together

In this final chapter, we will synthesize what we have studied. We will look at how to combine all of the approaches we've covered into a cohesive plan for awakening the subconscious mind. We'll also talk about how to keep a happy subconscious mindset and keep making great changes in our life.

Putting It All Together: How to Reach Your Objectives. We frequently get lost in the details when it comes to reaching our goals. We make plans, construct to-do lists, and try to stay focused, yet it sometimes feels as if we're not making any headway. In truth, reaching our objectives entails more than simply checking off chores. Understanding our motivation, setting realistic goals, and remaining dedicated to the process are all important.

Here are some pointers to help you put it all together and achieve your objectives:

- **Set explicit, attainable goals:**Begin by outlining your goals in a clear, specific, and attainable manner. Instead of just declaring, "I want to lose weight," specify a particular goal, such as "I want to lose 10 pounds in the next three months." Make sure your objectives are attainable and realistic in relation to your time and resources.

- **Recognize your motivation:**To stay focused on your objectives, you must first understand why you want to attain them. Do you want to improve your health? Obtain financial stability? Do you want to advance in your career? Knowing what motivates you might help you stay focused and devoted even when things are difficult.

- **Develop a plan:**Create a plan to achieve your goals after you've established them and recognized your motivation. Divide your aim into smaller, doable activities and assign deadlines to each one. Make sure your plan is adaptable enough to change as needed while being organized enough to keep you on track.

- **Track your progress:**Tracking your progress on a regular basis might help you keep motivated and focused. Keep track of your progress in a notebook or app, and celebrate minor triumphs along the way. Remember that growth isn't always linear, so don't let setbacks or sluggish progress discourage you.

- **Stay accountable:**Sharing your goals with others can help you stay on track. Consider joining a support group, collaborating with a friend or family member, or engaging a coach to assist you in staying on track. Accountability can also help you stay motivated when you want to quit.

- **Stay committed:**It takes time, work, and dedication to achieve your goals. There will be challenges and setbacks along the way, but it is critical to remain committed to the process. Remind yourself of your motivation and applaud each small step forward.

It takes time and effort to put everything together, but it's well worth it when you reach your goals. Remember to be focused, devoted, and to enjoy each step forward.